W9-BMK-399

Date: 11/18/15

J 591.77 WAL
Walters, Peter,
The hungriest mouth in the
sea /

PALM BEACH COUNTY
LIBRARY SYSTEM
3650 Summit Boulevard
West Palm Beach, FL 33406-4198

THE HUNGRIEST MOUTH IN THE SEA

IN THE SEA

BY PETER WALTERS

Far from the north, an island can be found.
Earth's salty seas flow all around.

But who has the hungriest mouth
in the seas of the South?

Floating out at sea, a cloud of green plankton drifts with the tide, soaking up the sun.

But look—a hungrier mouth
in the seas of the South!

Who would you say is heading this way?

Perhaps it's a seahorse with a pot-belly,
or the trailing tentacles of a moon jelly?

No, no, no, it's nothing like that.
It's someone else in this habitat.

But who can it be?

It's a pink Antarctic krill hunting in the sea!

Rising from the deep, a swarm of kicking krill
moves as one with unquestionable skill.

But look—a hungrier mouth
in the seas of the South!

Who would you say is heading this way?

Perhaps it's a petrel diving out of the skies,
or maybe a squid with enormous eyes?

No, no, no, it's nothing like that.
It's someone else in this habitat.

But who can it be?

It's a blue cod hunting in the sea!

Through the giant kelp, swims a shoal of cod —
an underwater forest, how very odd!

But look—a hungrier mouth
in the seas of the South!

Who would you say is heading this way?

Perhaps it's a swordfish swiping its prey,
or the poisonous spine of long-tail ray?

No, no, no, it's nothing like that.
It's someone else in this habitat.

But who can it be?

It's a yellow-eyed penguin hunting in the sea!

Diving under rocks, a raft of feathered penguins glides with bird wings instead of fishy fins.

But look—a hungrier mouth
in the seas of the South!

Who would you say is heading this way?

Perhaps it's a barracuda with silvery skin,
or maybe the mask of a Hector's dolphin?

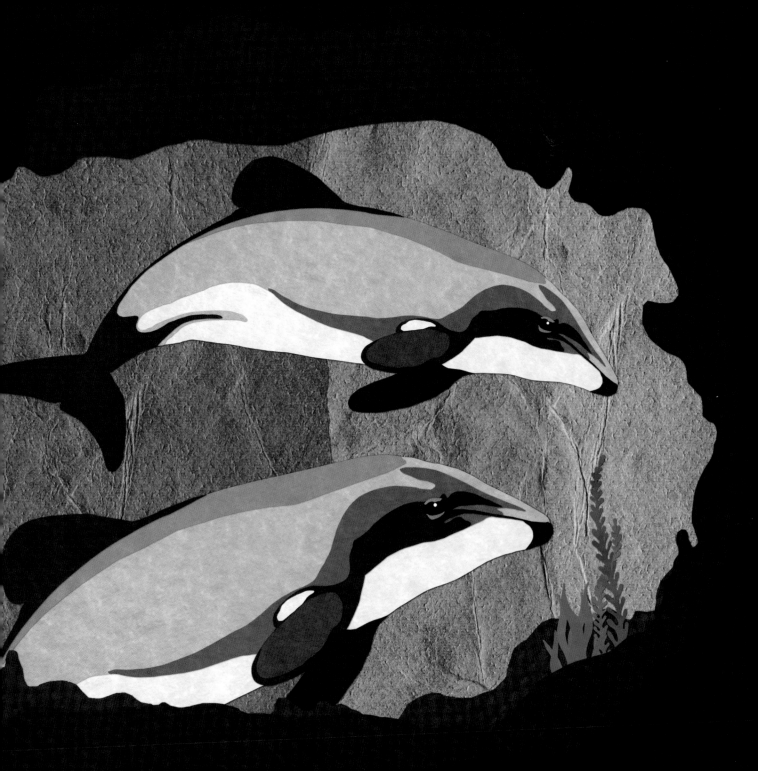

No, no, no, it's nothing like that.
It's someone else in this habitat.

But who can it be?

It's a brown fur seal hunting in the sea!

Flapping in the water, a herd of furry seals feeds in the bay, happy with their meals.

But look—a hungrier mouth
in the seas of the South!

Who would you say is heading this way?

Perhaps it's a great white shark with hundreds of teeth,
or maybe a sperm whale from cold waters beneath?

No, no, no, it's nothing like that.
It's someone else in this habitat.

But who can it be?

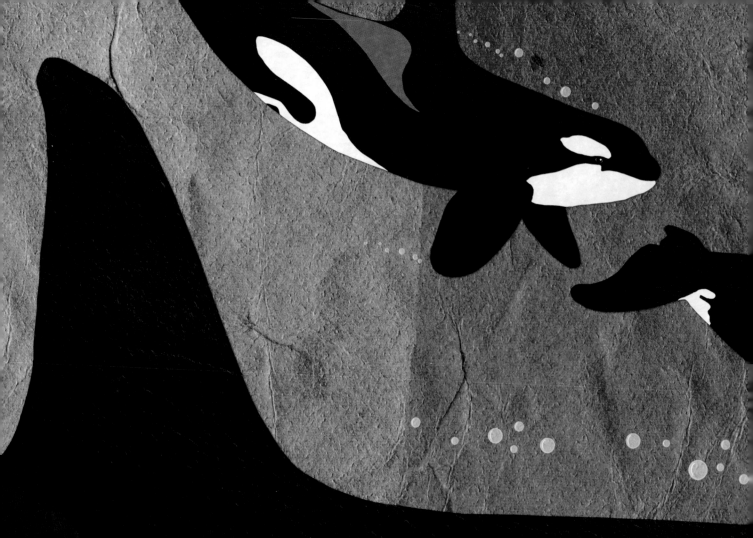

It's a black and white orca hunting in the sea!

Working on a team, with its mammal brain,
this hungry mouth tops the food chain.

Jumping from the sea, an awesome orca whale brings, with a splash, an end to this tale.

For Creative Minds

This For Creative Minds educational section contains activities to engage children in learning while making it fun at the same time. The activities build on the underlying subjects introduced in the story. While older children may be able to do these activities on their own, we encourage adults to work with the young children in their lives. Even if the adults have long forgotten or never learned this information, they can still work through the activities and be experts in their children's eyes! Exposure to these concepts at a young age helps to build a strong foundation for easier comprehension later in life. This section may be photocopied or printed from our website by the owner of this book for educational, non-commercial uses. Cross-curricular teaching activities for use at home or in the classroom, interactive quizzes, and more are available online. Go to www.ArbordalePublishing.com and click on the book's cover to explore all the links.

Marine Mammals

A **mammal** is any animal that has a backbone, is warm-blooded, breathes air, has hair, and produces milk for its young. A **marine mammal** is a mammal that spend most or all of its life in the ocean. Marine mammals live all around the world. The maps below show the range in yellow for each of the four marine mammals in this book.

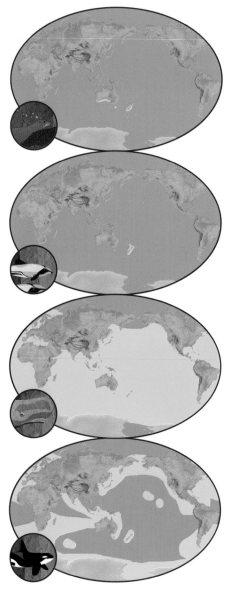

New Zealand fur seals are also called kekeno. They are an **endangered species**. This means that if people don't help them, they might disappear forever (**extinct**). Kekeno weigh up to 330 pounds (150 kg).

How much do you weigh? How much heavier or lighter is a kekeno than you are?

Hector's dolphins are also endangered. There are only 7,000 left in the world. Hector's dolphins are the smallest type of dolphin in the world. They grow to only 5 feet, 3 inches (1.6 m) long.

How tall are you? Is a Hector's dolphin longer or shorter than you are tall? By how much?

Sperm whales grow up to 60 feet (18 m) long—bigger than a school bus! When searching for food deep underwater, sperm whales can hold their breath for 90 minutes.

How long can you hold your breath? How much longer can a sperm whale hold its breath than you can hold yours?

Orcas, also known as killer whales, live in groups called **pods**. A single pod can have up to 40 whales. Orcas use teamwork to hunt with their pods and take down large prey. Adult orcas eat 375 pounds (170 kg) of food each day.

Humans eat an average of 5 pounds (2.25 kg) of food per day. How many days would it take for a person to eat as much as an orca does in one day?

Predator and Prey Matching

A **predator** is an animal that hunts other animals for food. Animals eaten by predators are called **prey**. Many animals are both predator and prey. Match each prey on the top of the page to its hungry predator on the bottom. Answers are below.

1. phytoplankton

2. yellow-eyed penguin

3. blue cod

4. Antarctic krill

5. New Zealand fur seal

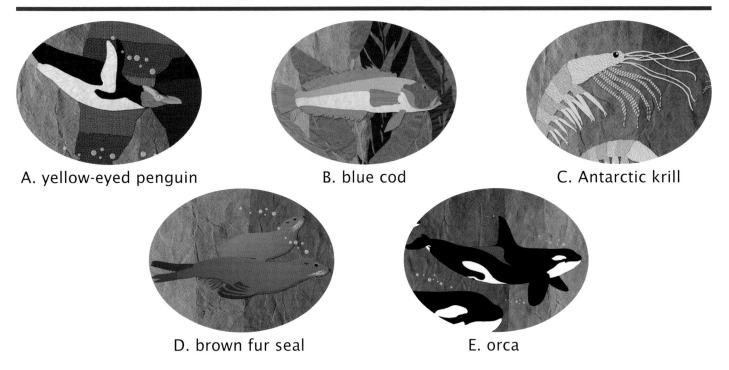

A. yellow-eyed penguin

B. blue cod

C. Antarctic krill

D. brown fur seal

E. orca

Answers: 1-C. 2-D. 3-A. 4-B. 5-E.

Food Web Cards

Copy or download this page and cut out the food web cards. Using the information in the book and on the card, stack each "**predator**" card on top of its "**prey**" card (predators eat the prey). How many cards can you get in one pile?

An animal with no natural predators is called an **apex predator**. Is there an apex predator here that is always at the top of your pile or on top of the food web?

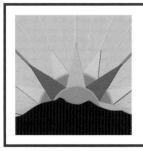

Sun

Provides energy for phytoplankton and other plants to grow

(bottom card)

Phytoplankton

Prey: gets its energy from the sun

Predators: krill

Krill

Prey: phytoplankton

Predators: jellyfish, seabird, small fish, squid, stingray

Jellyfish

Prey: krill

Predators: large fish, small fish, seabird

Stingray

Prey: krill

Predators: shark

Small Fish

Prey: krill, squid, jellyfish

Predators: large fish, penguin, seabird, seal, shark, squid

Seabird

Prey: jellyfish, krill, small fish, squid

Predators: orca, shark

Squid

Prey: krill, small fish

Predators: orca, large fish, penguin, seabird, seal, small fish

Penguin

Prey: small fish, squid

Predators: orca, seal, shark

Large Fish

Prey: jellyfish, small fish, squid

Predators: orca, seal, shark

Seal

Prey: large fish, penguins, small fish, squid

Predators: orca, shark

Shark

Prey: large fish, penguin, seabird, seal, small fish, stingray

Predators: orca

Orca

Prey: large fish, penguin, seabird, seal, shark, squid

Predators: none

Hungriest Mouth Games

Copy and cut out the food web cards.

Card game: If you have 2-3 players, use one set of cards. For 4-6 players, use two sets. Shuffle all the cards together and deal 4 cards to each player. Place extra cards in a draw pile. On your turn, say to one other player, "My (predator) eats your (prey)." If they have that prey, they give it to you and you add the card to your hand, then it is the next player's turn. If the person does not have the card you asked for, they take one card from the draw pile. The player with the most cards in their hand wins.

Conga line: For large groups, print out enough sets to give everyone a card. Attach your card to your shirt or wear it as a necklace with some yarn. Find your prey and "eat" them. When you eat someone, they stand behind you and hold onto your shoulders. The more people you eat, the longer your line becomes. If someone eats you, then you and everyone in your line must join their line. The winner is the predator with the longest line.

For Eliot—PW
Thanks to Jack Cover and Kate Rowe, General Curator and Media Relations Manager at the National Aquarium, for reviewing the accuracy of the information in this book.

Library of Congress Cataloging-in-Publication Data

Walters, Peter, 1984- author, illustrator.
  The hungriest mouth in the sea / by Peter Walters.
     pages cm
  Audience: Ages 4-8
  ISBN 978-1-62855-631-5 (english hardcover) -- ISBN 978-1-62855-636-0 (english pbk.) -- ISBN 978-1-62855-646-9 (english downloadable ebook) -- ISBN 978-1-62855-656-8 (english interactive dual-language ebook) -- ISBN 978-1-62855-641-4 (spanish pbk.) -- ISBN 978-1-62855-651-3 (spanish downloadable ebook) -- ISBN 978-1-62855-661-2 (spanish interactive dual-language ebook) 1. Marine animals--Food--Juvenile literature. 2. Food chains (Ecology)--Juvenile literature. 3. Predation (Biology)--Juvenile literature. I. Title.
  QL122.2.W355 2015
  591.77--dc23
                    2015009087

Translated into Spanish: *La boca más hambrienta del mar*

Lexile® Level: AD 670L
key phrases for educators: food web, ocean habitat, predator/prey, rhythm or rhyme,

Bibliography

New Zealand Department of Conservation. *Conservation*. Web. Accessed March 2015.
Te Ara - The Encyclopedia of New Zealand. Web. Accessed March 2015.
World Wildlife Fund New Zealand. Web. Accessed March 2015.
ARKive Wildlife Record. Web. Accessed March 2015.
Dingle, Hutchinson; Mckay; Schodde; Tait; and Vogt Cooke. *Encyclopedia of Animals: A Complete Visual Guide*. Weldon Owen, 2008. Print.

Manufactured in China, June 2015
This product conforms to CPSIA 2008
First Printing

Arbordale Publishing
Mt. Pleasant, SC 29464
www.ArbordalePublishing.com

Copyright 2015 © by Peter Walters

The "For Creative Minds" educational section may be copied by the owner for personal use or by educators using copies in classroom settings